Contents

Increasing affluence and a second-hand car allowed the author a geographical range previously denied to him and with various pals he embarked in the 1970s and 1980s on numerous expeditions to various parts of the country. There were busy main line centres to be explored – York, Doncaster, Crewe and the rest but also obscure corners that could only be found by recourse to maps, sometimes inquiring of locals with barely understandable dialects, after the fashion of Stanley inching his way into the Dark Heart of Africa.

He puts it: 'I have been a railway enthusiast for most of my life and was even watching trains from the pram, pushed by my older sister Jean to the local railway line in Weybridge, Surrey all those years ago. Serious 'number taking' came in 1959 until life changed, like so many of us, in the mid-1960s with popular music, dawning awareness of the opposite sex and under age drinking, though I did keep all my Ian Allan *abc* number books, known as *Combined Volumes* and colloquially as 'combines'. Although a man of steam, those 'combines' do have a good amount of diesel and electric numbers underlined.

'Memories from those days include the introduction of the Deltics; the Westerns under construction at Swindon Works; D4 GREAT GABLE on Camden running shed and a school visit to The Romney Hythe and Dymchurch Railway in September 1960 when the rail journeys between Waterloo East and Folkestone were behind one of the new BRC&W D6500s even though the Kent Coast line still had steam operation.

'In November 1971, in a nostalgic moment, I purchased the current Ian Allan Combined Volume. It dawned on me that there was still a lot of interest in 'train spotting' even though steam had finished on British Railways in August 1968 and despite, in the meantime, the hobby's precipitous decline, to become the butt of second-rate comedians' jokes. Thus my railway interest was reborn, the curtain going up with a visit to Woodhams scrap yard, Barry, South Wales on a special train on March 4 1972. On the way, instinct (or maybe 'learned behaviour') took over and I was soon noting down the diesel numbers, 'copping' (it was important to keep the jargon alive!) D1660 CITY OF TRURO at Swindon and D60 LYTHAM ST. ANNES at Cardiff. Our return journey was via the Central Wales Line, behind EE Type 3 (class 37) 6885, but it proved unequal to the task and (seemingly in protest) caught fire and shuddered to a halt near Llanwrtyd Wells where, somewhat alarmingly, we were surrounded by snow. Rescue eventually came in the form of Brush Type 4 (class 47) 1857 which propelled us as far as Llandrindod Wells where 1853 awaited to take over the train leaving 1857 to deal with 6885. I had returned to the rail tour scene with a vengeance. 'What really helped with photographing diesels and electrics all over the United Kingdom was meeting Don and Pat Brookes on holiday in Devon in 1974; they invited me to stay whenever I was in Co. Durham. So in August 1975 I took up the invite and stayed with them for the Stockton & Darlington 150 celebrations and returned every year for the next thirty years, along with other friends which resulted in trips all over Northern England and Scotland and a good number of photographs taken on these holidays make up the contents of this book.

'*Chasing Diesels* is a temporary departure in the *Diesel Dawn* series which is otherwise chiefly concerned with the development and early days of the Modernisation Plan diesels. The Editor has kindly indulged me in this present flight of nostalgia; well, it was a sort of *Diesel Dawn* for me! I'm told the series reverts to type next time with the Brush Type 2, or class 31 as we better know it.'

SETTLE and CARLISLE

To repeat myself, it was meeting Don and Pat Brookes in 1974 and their invite to stay with them in Co. Durham that meant I was able to travel so widely. Often I brought a friend and in the earlier days it was Steve Linney. It's terrifying now to reflect that much of it took place getting on for half a century ago! On June 22 1976 I drove our little party (Don, Pat, Steve and yours truly) over the Pennines on the A66 via Stainmore Summit. It was my first visit to the Settle and Carlisle, a line which in later years I was to travel on and 'lineside' quite a bit. Taking the A685 we ended up at Kirkby Stephen and I was surprised by the climb that is needed to reach Kirkby Stephen West, now happily open again for passengers. On parking up we could see the semaphores were set for both up and down routes and my first train on the S&C was a class 25 on an up freight. My first photograph on the S&C was this down working, a class 47 with just two wagons, the first with coal though I am not sure what the second one carried. It was a far cry indeed from the days of 4Fs, 8Fs and 9Fs on long coal trains but we were grateful for such crumbs.

Although we had a busy day planned we did not have to wait too long for this class 40 on an up freight to pass through; the first wagons look like bulk cement 'Presflos'.

On the way back we called in at Garsdale where we found a friendly signalman quite willing to let us have his thoughts and hopes for the future of the S&C. At this time there were rumours of its closure as a through route and it was widely regarded as doomed. As I drove back I noted the signals were off for a down working and for the third time today we were rewarded with a freight working, a bulk cement train headed by a pair of class 25s.

I headed north again with Steve for a few days in November 1976 and bonfire night (or rather the fleeting hours of daylight before it) found us once again on the S&C – famously described as 'crossing the roof of the Pennines'. At Appleby station we found 25044 at the head of a block train of cement and 25111 shunting the yard. This was a stranger from Eastfield, something of a scoop for Don. The old 'boundaries' for locomotives were rapidly breaking down and gone were the days when an engine kept strictly to a particular line – he saw it again the following summer working empty stock at Euston! This was something inconceivable before 1968. We then headed down to Kirkby Stephen West station via Warcop. Our plan was to see two of the through passenger trains of the day; the first was due off Appleby at 13.00 for Nottingham and at 13.17 Holbeck's 45029 appeared and with a wave from the train crew was soon gone. The route indicators on locomotives now were fixed at 0000.

Taking the B6259 we headed for Ais Gill Summit and there is plenty of space to park a car here. We knew there was a down passenger due and were rewarded for our patience as Ais Gill signalbox must have been switched out. The signals accordingly stayed at clear throughout our visit, during which 45039 THE MANCHESTER REGIMENT appeared on a Carlisle-bound train.

We were rewarded soon after noting 45039 by 25175 on a down freight – according to my *Locoshed Book* of 1976 it was then a Cricklewood engine. This was of course the far south end of the Midland and while it was not an impossibility for a Cricklewood steam engine, a 4F 0-6-0 (in extremis) perhaps, to get this far north, such a phenomenon was much more likely with diesels.

Then we ventured up to the road bridge a short way off from Ais Gill Summit, to be rewarded this time with another freight, an unrecorded class 45 at the head of a motley collection of wagons; this is one of my favourite photos of the S&C and that includes a good number of steam subjects over the years, taken from this same vantage point. The night was spent with a bonfire and fireworks back at Crook along with a few of the neighbours. And the weather held out!

Friday 20 July 1978 saw another car ride out to the S&C and if you want to take photographs alongside this line it takes a few trips to reconnoitre the numerous vantage points. In 1977 we had found a lovely view looking down on the north portal of Blea Moor Tunnel, after a right-hand turn off the B6255. On a Carlisle-bound train was 40050 – note the banner repeater signal near the tunnel mouth.

This banner repeater signal was a help as we knew there was a passenger train due off Appleby at 14.02 and at Settle at 14.54 so I reckoned this would pass our vantage point at about 14.30. It had not appeared by 14.40; vigilance slackened and my timetabling skills brought into question so I had to bear a bit of leg pulling. However it was soon upon us, headed by 45019 (another Holbeck engine) the yellow front end very prominent and with a wave (at least it looked a wave) from the crew it disappeared into the murky depths of the tunnel.

Ais Gill Summit in July 1979 and once again the reward was a northbound freight, this time with 40121 at the front, then a Longsight-based locomotive. I'm no wagon aficionado but the examples here seem intriguing; a single mineral at the front, then what I always understood to be grain wagons, then containers of a distinctive livery, in steel opens.

During these expeditions to the north of England we always liked to spend a few hours on Carlisle Citadel as in those days nearly everything was loco-hauled and a good variety was almost guaranteed. There were plenty of Scottish diesels of course – like Eastfield's 27104 (D5387 that was) in the stabling point on the westside of the station.

A visit to Kingmoor yard north of Citadel was obligatory and today, 20 July 1978, was no exception. It was always easy to park overlooking the yard as there was little traffic about. On the up side the large area (to the right, now turned over to a nature reserve) once accommodated the mighty Kingmoor steam Motive Power Depot; the later diesel depot was on the opposite side of the running lines. This is the view looking north to the New Yard with 40027 and 40028 – specially pleasing for Don as he was trying to photograph as many of the class as he could before they were all withdrawn. Well, each to his own...

Consett Steel Works

Friday August 1 1980 was a long day as we drove all the back from Boat of Garten, Scotland to where Don lived in Crook, Co. Durham. On nearing Corbridge the bad weather left us and on joining the A68 the sun came out but it was not a happy place we were going to. The A692 led to Consett where the steel works were closed the same month, with the certain prospect of high unemployment. The coke ovens were burning and we were able to get a number of photographs from the over bridge including a fair number of wagons and BSC diesel shunters. As we left another car load of people pulled up with the same idea; it was a sad place though, and I wanted to leave.

A diesel shunter still in use at the works. Only one of these yellow-liveried 0-6-0s survived the closure and the remainder were scrapped soon after. Where we stayed in Crook is a few hundred feet above sea level and our friends then lived in the middle of a row of terraced houses (Low Jobs Hill) above Crook. On a clear summer evening at the back of the house an orange glow lit up the sky in the distance, but no more after this month.

Newcastle

Although I spent many holidays in Co. Durham I inexplicably paid very few visits to Newcastle station; well, living near the ECML Don had 'seen everything' but this Wednesday June 23 1976 we took a quick drive to Durham and a dmu ride to Newcastle, resulting in a few photos. This one was taken from the south end of the station with 37066 (D6768) within spitting distance of its home depot of Gateshead on a through freight.

One of the things I did enjoy during my earlier visits to the North East was coming across a number of class 03 diesels for the first time, before they all disappeared. Among these was 03059 (D2059) on pw duties, burbling away while track workers got down to it in the background.

I must admit I have never been a big fan of the Deltics, indeed I have never ridden behind one though at the time with the introduction of the HSTs it was obvious that the class 55s had a limited future so it would have been wrong not to photograph one or two, including this anonymous example. Not only had I managed to visit Newcastle Central, but also the 'Caravette Centre of the North'!

Tinsley

Tinsley was a depot I at last managed to visit, complete with permit, on Saturday 15 October 1983. I say at last because a year before I had arranged a permit with some friends but on the very morning developed sciatica, very painful and was off work for two weeks. Today my good friend Graham Ward drove me and my nephew Paul up to Sheffield and once in the area I got us lost; I've never been the best at navigating. We left the M1 at Jct. 34 and drove around only to arrive at Jct.33; back to Jct.34; found ourselves at Brinsworth; drove under the motorway and miraculously found ourselves at the depot entrance! Parked the car in the staff car park and presented ourselves at the Foreman's office and ended up with a very helpful guide. He showed us a class 37 on rails sinking into the ash; the place was largely built on made up ground consisting mainly of this power station by-product and the track had to be dug up and repacked. He also informed us that locomotives had to mount a severe gradient just to access the main building. There were six bays at each end (it was split into two, an east and a west end) and this shot shows one of the class 56s then based at Tinsley in one of the bays at the side. Each bay held just two engines, an arrangement which reduced the likelihood of an engine being 'blocked' by another under repair. At the same time we caught 56125, then new, leave the depot for what I believe was acceptance trials. Our guide, who had started his career on the Pennine Electrics didn't think to much of the class 56s, declaring that they 'needed too much maintenance and wore parts out to quickly'. Needless to say, this was an 'unofficial' view.

One end of the depot – east or west I'm not sure) with the six lines running in and our guide peering at something – a worn-out class 56 part perhaps? On looking more closely at this slide I noticed a former steam locomotive tender on the left – presumably for the storage and disposal of something noxious – used sump oil or suchlike? The weather was awful but a number of the faithful were by the fence noting down what they could see and must have been wondering how we managed to get round. Well this was my only visit to Tinsley which had been demolished by April 1999. Few of these new modern depots lasted long.

There were a good number of diesels on shed on Saturday 15 October 1983 and this line up was fairly typical – classes 20, 31, 37, 45 and 47 and note the different headcode panels on the two class 37s. This is what we saw:
08208 08219 08335 08389 08434 08485 08492 08507 08510 08543 08749 08877 08879
all based at Tinsley.

13001 one of the master and slave units (formerly 4501)
20004 20008 20009 20010 20054 20076 20088 20092 20096 20105 20145 20128 20209
25234 25235
31131 31235 31283
37014 37048 37092 37104 37113 37246
47316 47566
40196
45019 45026 45038 45040 45048 45063
46017
56006 56016 56021 56022 56025 56074 56090 56093 56096 56101 56102 56104 56124

Thirsk

After a few days in Crook, Tuesday 19 July 1978 saw a good time at the North Yorkshire Moors Railway and on the way it was decided to stop off at Thirsk station – apparently a Deltic was due. The station had seen better days – the main line platforms had been removed, just the slow line platforms were in use and fenced off from the fast running lines. We were lucky because in the space of a few minutes were able to photograph 47430, 47550 and 55013 THE BLACK WATCH (shown here). What I did not realise at the time that in less than three years this photograph would be history and the HSTs would have replaced the Deltics.

Sunday 22 August 1982 was the last full day of a holiday in Crook. A couple of months previously I had written off for a number of shed permits; belying national stereotypes, those we used in Scotland had been free but the two we used today cost £1.15p a head and the first one was for the small diesel shed at Darlington. Time of visit today was for 11.30pm and after setting off from Crook Don navigated us into the staff car park right next to the site of the former steam shed (one of Don's former haunts) and he told us of times walking along line after line of engines and of the long road at the back where every weekend different engines were lined up ready for the Works. We crossed a footbridge to get access to the well-lit depot that serviced the local dmus. The foreman was vastly amused that we should want to visit his depot; Don had never been here though on chatting to one of the cleaning ladies found he had been at school with her daughter. The diesels lined up here were local shunters 08063, 08159, 08161, 08225, 08268, 08506 and 08774 along with 31285 and 37045 which was a new one for me. This photo shows 08268 and 08774 at home.

A general view of the clean and neat five road depot which was probably a better place to work than the old steam shed – though it provided for far fewer jobs. Architecturally, funnily enough, it was closely similar to the steam shed, built back in LNER days. This depot did not have much longer; it was closed in 1984 when its work was transferred to Thornaby and the tracks lifted by mid-1985.

Miscellany

37006 at Thornaby, the giant steam shed designed to accommodate diesels and electrics within a few years, on that Sunday, 22 August. The place was an old favourite, where we were always allowed quite a bit of freedom: Don wanted to do his own thing while John wrote the numbers down for us and I took mostly black and white photos. On visits here I always found the staff to be very friendly though traffic had clearly lessened since steam days. Not so many engines were required, presumably and the roundhouse was slowly reverting to nature! Thornaby yielded thirteen 08 shunters, some of which were new to me; eighteen class 31s, seven class 37s, three class 40s, nine class 47s including 47212 which left me with only ten more to see – the numbers bug had returned more virulent than ever! The day was completed by visits to West Hartlepool and Sunderland. West Hartlepool stabling point closed in April 1983; Sunderland sadly followed in April 1994. The last driver to sign on for duty at Thornaby did so on Saturday, December 8 2007.

During our exploits in North East England Steve and I would often indulge in a spontaneous break for somewhere of railway interest but off the beaten track as it were. Spontaneous is probably not quite the right word, for some element of planning was necessary to mitigate my lack of spatial awareness. In June 1976 (that famous year of sunshine) we went looking for the Philadelphia coal mining complex in Co. Durham, hoping in particular for some class 14s, sold off (or more or less given away with a measure of relief) by BR some years before. We were made welcome by the local staff who arranged for one of their locomotives to be positioned for us. As you can see, while it was indeed a former BR diesel, it was a common-or-garden 08, carrying the running number 510. We hid our disappointment and thanked the staff for their help. I rather like the contrast – solid outline versus the squat 'beetle'. Oddly, both designs (when you think about it) derived from the pre-War years.

Chasing Diesels

On Friday 26 June 1976, inevitably another hot day, it was time to drive home and on the way we called in at another steelworks, at Corby, not too far off the A1, our main route home. We were looking for the class 14s again and found two of them at work. After a good deal of pleading with security staff (or 'guards' as we called them) Steve was allowed to photograph No.49 amid the everyday stuff of a working colliery, using my camera. Former D9547 did not survive, as it was cut up at Corby in August, 1982.

Monday July 25 1977 was the first day of the annual holiday in Crook, so to break the drive north up the A1 a stop at Doncaster station seemed attractive enough. The platform ticket machine would not accept our 2p (yes, 2p!) coins but thanks to a helpful member of staff it was eventually persuaded to cough up our tickets. It was my first visit to Doncaster station but Steve had been before and wandered off for a coffee fix in the buffet. I mooched around taking a few photos; we were hoping to come across one of the new class 56s being built at Doncaster and it turned out we were in luck – brand spanking 56033 suddenly appeared from the Works and I had to rush and get Steve who nearly choked on his coffee! Well we got our first photo of a class 56 looking smart in its BR livery.

We travelled home on Sunday 31 July and made a point of dropping in at Knottingley depot which is not too far off the A1. Several class 47s can be seen on shed here – their purpose was to work Merry go Round trains to at least three power stations in the area. None was actually allocated here (though in ways effectively they were) but the depot did have a number of shunters. We never got 'past the wire' and there was a similar result the following year but although we were not allowed round we were given a list of the diesels on shed.

Don took us to various sites in Co. Durham where diesel shunters were left over the weekend to save travelling back to their home depot. On Saturday 15 July 1978 we drove into Darlington but on the way Don navigated us to the rubbish tip at Witton-le-Wear, not far from Crook where we found and photographed 03067. This was one of a number (a first for me) working from Gateshead depot. I think the warning notice speaks for itself, though we were the only people present, it being a weekend. After all, it was hardly a beauty spot.

Another aim that day was a ride to Saltburn by dmu, a bit of 'track bashing' – we'd never been on the line and the fare was only 94p single adult. While at Darlington Bank Top station 55013 THE BLACK WATCH pulled in on this London-bound train. On board the dmu we got the seats behind the driver and as we headed for the branch 55007 PINZA appeared on a down train; a shot from inside the dmu failed dismally but yes we did pass Thornaby depot and managed to note locally based 08864, 31282, 37193 and 47360 and a visitor from Gateshead, 47430.

Saturday 28 July 1979 was the day Steve and I drove home after another pleasant holiday in the North East and a weekend break in Scotland at Boat of Garten, all in my trusty white Austin Allegro XPB 186N and yes it did have the square steering wheel. I still marvel at the distance I covered in this car. Today we looked for the stabling point at Worksop; I ventured up a rough track and we found 08824 from Shirebrook and 56005 and 56015 but stayed in the car for photography as we were in a rush to get home and still had to find the closed station at Mansfield, which is another story.

Now forward a few years to Sunday 24 July 1983 and another friend was holidaying with me in Crook, John Stonard, who for many years worked on West Byfleet station and sadly died a few years ago. Today was a Sunday and we were bound for various depots in Scotland along with Don – an early start. Our final call of the day was Carstairs station where we found 20086, 20127 and 27211 on the stabling point while 26002 worked in on a train of vans. Well we fancied a short piece of linesiding, it being a very good day weather-wise, so we drove along some country roads and ended up at a bridge near Thankerton where there had once been a station, closed to passengers on 4 January 1965. Once the car was parked we heard a diesel, so grabbed the cameras; Don ran down some stairs but missed 40131 at the head of a down ballast train though as you can see, I didn't.

Then I noticed there was a class 20 banking this ballast train and I shouted at Don hoping he heard and would get a shot. I managed a half-decent picture of 20197. This is the only time I have witnessed banking on the WCML and we were very lucky to see this train let alone photograph it.

SOUTHERN ENGLAND

I spent a few days in the New Forest in the July of the blazing year, 1976. It wasn't quite as enchanting as it sounds, for it was a family 'do' with nieces, nephews and cousins dossing on mattresses and sharing a room. In between family events (or the avoiding of some) I managed a few stolen railway moments on the Fawley branch. It had closed to passengers in 1966 but oil trains still ran to and from the Fawley Oil Terminus. On 15 July I was lucky enough to catch 33023 waiting to leave Fawley station with an oil train. Derry's luck was holding out, for 33029 then arrived on a train of empty oil tanks.

September 9 1976. The remarkable summer went on though I recall the rains came in September – the very day my friend Ian Sixsmith finally managed to get away on holiday that year! Happily I had a number of summer holidays at Avonwick station on the former Kingsbridge branch in South Devon, then run by Bob Gale and his wife and for this late summer holiday I took my good friend John Stonard. We decided on a ride from Plymouth to Penzance and the BR Awayday fare for me was £3.24p and cheaper for John. Our train from Plymouth was headed by 50030, the 7.30am from Paddington, a lovely journey through Cornwall and a first for me. At Plymouth North Road I was able to record Laira's 08488 trundling along with what must have been a trip freight from the Cornish direction. A most interesting journey through Cornwall with the beautiful infrastructure and semaphore signals resulted in an unnoticed minute late arrival at Penzance. Here (below) I was able to photograph one of the disappearing Westerns, 1010 WESTERN CAMPAIGNER running down to pick up a parcels train. Happily this locomotive only resides a few miles from where I now live in Minehead, at Williton, West Somerset. The return journey was behind 50030 though we would have preferred 1010.

Another journey west the next day saw us at Par station. 08052 in thoroughly pannier tank tradition, was on a short freight train and at the back of the down main platform was Laira's 25052. This was unremarkable enough but once the 08 had passed another class 25 was revealed (below) at the other end of the very short train – presumably it was a pw working of some sort. There was no chance to get the number – we were on our return train pulling in to Par station. This is a fine memory as it was my last ordinary ride behind a Western – 1033 WESTERN TROOPER.

16 April 1977. Stephen Linney, a friend of over fifty years and I spent a few days in Devon at Avonwick station again, a year later and this was our last full day before returning home on the Sunday. I had taken charge of the aforementioned second-hand Austin Allegro and was still coming to terms with the square steering wheel. Today we travelled around the West Country principally to get some photos of 33104 and 33106 working the 'Thames Tamar Express' organised by the Merchant Navy Preservation Society. One port of call was Lostwithiel station where sadly the down side buildings had been demolished and replaced by a bus shelter though happily the signalbox and lower quadrant semaphore signals were still there. The bonus was 25216 rumbling away in the station yard – a number of them had replaced the Western Region diesel hydraulic Hymeks. After the special had passed we chased it back to Plymouth and parked near Laira diesel depot (below). We were able to look down on the running lines and got into conversation with a local who remembered steam and kept us entertained with tales of those days. We also were in the company of others awaiting the special though we also had the regular traffic passing by which included 47537 on this passenger train.

Laira diesel depot was quite remarkable in its modernity, owing much in its styling to post-War construction on the SNCF. The high hall was necessary for the cranes used to remove/replace engines from the diesel hydraulics operated by the depot. During the wait for the special we had marked a back way into the depot for a closer look (below) at this old tender; dmu power car W55015 and D1009 minus name and number plates. I must admit we did not try to get round the rest of the shed, I doubt whether we would have got very far.

October 1 1977. This Saturday morning required a 7.30am start from Weybridge with Steve Linney for company as we wanted to get to St Pancras where, unbelievably though it might sound now, if you arrived early there would be parking spaces available. 44005 was due to depart at 9am with a farewell tour for the class 44 (44008 and 44009 were also involved) appropriately named the Peaks Express. The itinerary included Manchester Piccadilly and an evening return by 9pm. Sadly we had very little time to get our photos and were not pleased with the result. However once the special had departed we were able to witness 45144 ROYAL SIGNALS leave, to much better effect.

Chasing Diesels

The Southern Region post-steam was not notable for numbers or variety of locomotives, so we were rather lucky on November 20 1977 to come across shunter 09001 stabled along with electro-diesel 73105 at the east end of Woking station. Moreover 09020 was working in the goods yard, diesel 33001 worked through on an Exeter train; also noted were 33011 33027 and 73154. I've chosen the better photographic results here: electro-diesel 73114 (above) is heading a pw train in the down direction while below, 73003 and 33055 are on the stabling point at the up side just short of the up platform which served slow trains to London. It's nostalgic to recall the Lamb's Navy Rum advert, long ago banned on at least two grounds.

August 26 1978 was the Saturday of a bank holiday weekend and Don and I had a challenging drive to Kent in dense traffic. By the time we reached Pembury vehicles were at a near standstill so it was out with the map and along the B2010, B2163 and the A20 to get to Folkestone but the result for SR locomotives was a big zero. A rare map reading triumph wasted. On to Dover where the reward (after a trek uphill) was this pair of electro-diesels, 73117 and 73119.

Then in the Marine station area we found former D6500 Type 3s 33039 and 33052 – these sidings stand on the easternmost end of the yard of the old Dover steam MPD; its remains lie some distance beyond. Shunting in the then extensive yards were 08847, 09008 and 09019 outbased from Ashford but these were not amenable to photography.

Chasing Diesels

Our next destination that Saturday was Ashford for the stabling point alongside the station; with my usual driving skill I overshot the turn into the station car park and was dismayed to miss (I calculated) at least five locomotives. After negotiating the one way and safely berthing us in the car park, my estimate was found to be a bit out as we found nine locomotives stabled there; 08833, 33018, 33040, 33064, 33206, 73103, 73105, 73110 and 73138, all close together. Don wanted to spend a while on the station but time was getting on and we had to seek out Ashford Chart Leacon Works which we found with the aid of an OS map. We were greeted by a notice warning that engine spotters were only allowed in with a permit but very nicely positioned, complementing the skips, 71003 was in store outside – actually, at this time the whole class was in store. A drive alongside the depot revealed nothing but electric multiple units on shed.

Next on the day's agenda was Tonbridge, a town I was not familiar with but we found a car park near the station and while Don got the platform tickets it was the usual tale, an approaching train did not allow us time to get the cameras ready and we missed 33060 and 33202 heading a fully braked freight in the Ashford direction. The stabling point was in the fork of the Sevenoaks and Redhill lines west of the station, just as the Ian Allan *Shed Directory* said it was. We were able to see this from the station but it took a good half hour of driving round, mainly in and out of cul-de-sacs before eventually chancing upon the footpath that gave us this good view. We found a friendly member of staff busy sunning himself who not only let us round but got the signalman to give us the number of a diesel shunter parked there, 08380. We didn't stop too long as another, rather less friendly member of staff appeared so we contented ourselves with photographs from the footbridge. Our welcome had worn out. Noted today were 09011, 33207, 33209, 33210, 73003 and 73122.

The days were long, and we left Tonbridge at 5.30pm with plenty of light left, driving west on the A25 to Redhill and another diesel stabling point where once a busy steam MPD had been. In fact the tracks which served to stable a handful of diesels were remnants of the old MPD yard, in the fork of the lines to Brighton and Reading. Once again it took a while to find the way in to this place which was up the hill from the station near a bus terminus. We chanced upon another friendly BR bloke and under his guidance were able to note down 33033, 33035, 73112 and 73135, and to photograph 08376.

Next day, August 27 1978 we tried some London locations. Stewarts Lane as usual was a firm 'no'. It was impossible to 'wander in' here looking innocent, the entrance being a door in a wall. Hither Green never seemed to present a problem, for it was curiously deserted most of the time and a 'visitor' could have the place to himself. Indeed it got better on this occasion as the now familiar figure, the nice BR man, once again put in an appearance, enquiring if we 'were spotting trains?' Access to the depot (little changed since it was built for steam engines back in the 1930s) was off one of the platforms and down a path. Before that, a bonus appeared in the form of Canton's 47098 awaiting the road south with a freight train. The point is made again, such a situation would have been next to impossible in steam days – imagine a Canton Hall on a southbound freight at Hither Green in 1960! Another BR chap (they were everywhere that day!) directed us to the Foreman's office which

Chasing Diesels

was on the far side of the six road shed. As a precaution we noted everything we saw on a deliberately circuitous route to the Foreman but he was another pleasant sort who merely warned us to take care. Back then if you fell in a pit it was your own silly fault and no-one else's. On the shed were: 08375, 08760, 09004, 09010, 33046 (front end damage, see above), 33057, 33058, 33059, 33061, 33204, 33211, 73102, 73133 and 73136. The great days were obviously in the past somewhat; in the 1960s almost the entire class of D6500 Type 3 (class 33) diesels were allocated here and dozens could be found at times. Much to Don's delight there were four stored class 71: 71004, 71009, 71013 and 71014, stored on the east side of the shed alongside the staff car park. From these three views of class 33s inside, and the general view outside (below) the steam origins of the shed are obvious. The coaling stage (demolished) and the turntable (still there into the 1970s) in the view below were on made-up ground over on the right; the partition in the middle of the shed was erected in the 1950s to divide off the steam engines from the new, much more dirt-sensitive new diesels.

Electro-diesels on Hither Green shed that day – does that magnificent clock survive somewhere, still?

Brighton station on August 29 1978 and somehow I had managed to find the place without a map. On arrival in the car park I realised we were in the shadow of the former LBSCR works which closed in the late 1950s. Brighton is a very fine station but there was little worth photographing; 73135 was inside under that distinctive roof – how carefully the third rail is shielded for the staff.

Chasing Diesels

A second class 73, 73133 outside the station – a passing BR man wondered why we bothered to photograph these locomotives; for whatever reason, he was certainly not impressed by them!

My thirtieth birthday, August 30 1978, prompted a nostalgic return to old haunts, Haines Bridge in Weybridge, two minutes walk from home where I spent many times train spotting 1959-1963. A short time there in the afternoon brought 33001, 33014 and 33028, light engine on the down slow line – a quite rare occurrence in my experience. In the evening, before a visit to the local, we returned and saw 33201 on the 19.01 Waterloo-Exeter. This was another rarity, to find a 33/2 on the South Western Section – I even informed *The Railway Magazine* which remained curiously unimpressed. We resisted the call of the ale just sufficiently to catch 33005 on an up Exeter working and then it was off to the late lamented *Duke of York*.

Friday September 9 1978 was an old fashioned spotting trip; a visit to some of the London terminus stations and a bit of a 'retrospective' – such a day was nothing new for me for in the early 1960s I (and thousands others of my ilk) would get a cheap (in my case 3/3d) return to Waterloo and then the Underground to Kings Cross, visit that station; up the steps to St Pancras (great memory of finding Holbeck's 70053 MORAY FIRTH there in 1961) then along the Euston Road to that windswept office block/shopping centre and afterwards spend the afternoon at Paddington where the Warships were taking over the work from the Castles and Kings. Today we caught the 09.54 from Weybridge and at Waterloo, the City line to Liverpool Street – hence Brush 31129 (then of March and probably filched by Stratford) on the stabling point, and 08958 serving as station pilot. This was a Stratford locomotive of course and both diesels were new to me, so – a good start to the day.

The lovely hall of St Pancras was usually very quiet and lacking in one important respect – trains, especially in the middle of the day. It was better on this occasion though and we found another Holbeck surprise, 45054 COLDSTREAM GUARDSMAN awaiting departure while another, Toton's 45117 arrived on a passenger train. The station pilot, Cricklewood's 08902 turned up as we left.

It is not easy to photograph inside the modern Euston though I had a good stab at class 87 87019 WINSTON CHURCHILL along with others stabled between turns. To an extent this was a leftover from steam days and now of course 'running round' a train and awaiting the next turn practically no longer exists. There were plenty of locomotives about including 25111, last seen at Appleby the previous November, 25173, 86013, 86016, 86024, 86214, 86221, 86234 and 86243. There was also a good number of class 87s, all (along with WINSTON CHURCHILL recalling names from various classes/company origins, with a distinctly 'Pacific' flavour: 87004 BRITANNIA, 87005 CITY OF LONDON, 87011 THE BLACK PRINCE, 87020 NORTH BRITON, 87025 BORDERER, 87030 BLACK DOUGLAS, 87031 HAL OF THE WYND AND 87033 THANE OF FIFE.

Swindon Interlude 1. We met at lunchtime at Swindon Works for a relaxed guided tour – it cost the princely sum of 30p – on February 5 1979 and it was particularly pleasing to see 6000 KING GEORGE V there, to me the most famous locomotive built at these late, lamented works. A good number of 08 diesel shunters were under repair on which included (above) 08398, actually based at Swindon shed. Nearby (below) was 03382 of Landore, no doubt receiving its last major attention at a BR Works.

Swindon Interlude 2. I had to include this view of the A shop/lifting shop which we have lost, a while after the Westerns had been withdrawn. 1041 WESTERN PRINCE was by now privately owned but able to receive attention from Swindon men who had worked on the class as part of their day to day job. Sadly outside shows the fate of most of the others – cabs of scrapped Westerns less than twenty years after their introduction. Why the cabs were separated like this and kept for a while, balanced on sleepers, is a mystery to me.

As declared, my real awakening, or re-awakening, to the railway hobby was a trip to the Woodham yard in Barry, South Wales. The landscape of the working railway was changing. There weren't so many locomotives to go after for a start and it was about this time that British Rail decided to renumber all their diesel and electric locomotives using the TOPS computer system; since the end of steam they had removed the D from diesels and the E from the electrics which had distinguished them from WR steam engines. On Saturday 22 May 1980 we took to the M4 aiming for three major diesel depots in South Wales. We easily found Severn Tunnel Junction station and you couldn't miss the depot. As the *Locoshed Directory* informed us: *Go straight ahead outside the station and turn sharp second left at the BRSA building into a drive which leads to the depot.* Walking time 10 minutes; we did it in under 5! Our first find was 08932 from Ebbw Junction TMD busying itself in the yard on the down side of the running lines. A member of staff allowed us to look around as long as we didn't cross any lines and in any case there was a road that took you right alongside the maintenance shed. Relations with the BR workforce continued in general amity! Back on the M4 we tried to find Ebbw Junction; no luck. Cardiff was by contrast straightforward; we rolled up at the main entrance at Canton, made a note of what we could see and then found a side road which led to the famous footbridge across the depot from which George Heiron took those remarkable photographs of serried ranks of ex-GW 4-6-0s, wreathed in steam. The steam origins of the main shed building is clear on the left there, as 47239 passes on an up freight.

Chasing Diesels

Looking west from the footbridge towards the station, Canton's steam antecedents became plainer than ever, with the water tank and remnants of the coal stage. On the footbridge (subsequently demolished, I read) we met a fellow enthusiast who gave us directions on how to find the elusive Ebbw Junction. For the interested, there follows a list of what we saw outside the depot and passing on the main line – no HSTs thank goodness. 08187, 08350, 08353 all Canton-based and happily a good number of class 37s; 37158, 37178 and 37192 some visitors from Landore further down the line while the remainder were all based at Canton. 37227, 37248, 37272, 37273, 37279, 37280, 37282, 37288, 37290, 37292 and 37294. Visitors from beyond the WR were: 45006 HONOURABLE ARTILLERY COMPANY, 45012 and 45142 all from Holbeck in Leeds. One thing about the class 45, when they were renumbered it was certainly not in numerical order, it seems to be random, perhaps on works visits? Class 46 was so dealt with in order and at the time were based at Canton, Gateshead and Laira; on shed today were 46013, 46018 and 46025. The majority of main line locomotives on use on the WR at this time, for mixed traffic, were the 47s and today we had 47029 from Laira while the following were all Canton: 47142, 47159, 47185, 47235 and 47240 with 47495 visiting from Landore. However there were some LMR-based ones, 47200 from Toton and 47249 and 47463 from Crewe. What we did not see today in South Wales were any Westerns.

Thanks to the knowledgeable fellow enthusiast from the footbridge, on our return journey we found Ebbw Junction, near the site of the former steam shed, by then an area of waste land. It turned out to be shows this four road maintenance depot . We encountered yet another friendly foreman who gave us the run of the place and though we asked him what he thought about class 56s being based in South Wales he diplomatically declined to comment.

Peeping over the parapet of the adjacent bridge revealed a couple of scruffy (were they ever not so?) shunters in equally scruffy surroundings. The main part of the depot is over on the left, across the South Wales main line. At one time Ebbw had over twenty 08 shunters for work in the surrounding district with some always out based at Newport Pill. (Today at Pill it was 08119, 08574, 08587 and 08634). Also shown is a good line up of 37s though none of them was based at Ebbw. On the main depot today were 08111, 08117, 08363, 08487, 08582, 08595, 08639, 08652, 08812 and 08822 all stabled for the weekend before work started again in earnest on Monday morning. 25032, 25077, 25155 and 25219 were all from Canton, transferred in as replacements for the Hymeks as the diesel hydraulics were got rid of. The class 37s on shed were split between Canton and Landore but as they were a common user locomotive I sometimes wondered if allocations really meant that much. Canton: 37162, 37186, 37213, 37214, 37222, 37230 and 37294. Landore based: 37159, 37231, 37233 and 37289. The main work for the class of course was coal, along with the steel and other materials associated with the giant Llanwern steel works. Just one 47 was encountered, Canton's own 47105. Homeward bound we called in briefly at Swindon and Don was rewarded with 1009 WESTERN INVADER which materialised on a train from the Gloucester direction; replacement of the class was nearly complete and the next three main line passenger trains to appear were hauled by 50026, 50045 and 50049.

I would probably not book a rail tour in January again! This one that pals Steven and Graham joined me on was 'The Welsh Wizard' organised by Railway Pictorial Publications Railtours, RPPR for short, on January 27 1979 which we were due to catch from Reading at 8.25. Well we had to bump start my car but got to Reading in good time and travelled behind 37228 and 50008, to Cardiff General and on to Tondu. Our first photo stop was here, Barry station in the snow, with some class 47s and shunters outside the old Barry Railway steam shed, converted to stable diesels. Tour participants simply wandered where they fancied! The Canton shunter in view, 08484, was formerly at Old Oak Common. Distantly, frozen in the background, are the mouldering Woodham yard steam locomotives awaiting rescue.

At Tondu Landore's 37183 and 37190 took over 'The Welsh Wizard'. Again the access is astonishing, by today's lights; we simply opened the doors and clambered down on to the track. Several decades on, there is no way I would attempt to climb down from a BR Mk.1 carriage!

The 'Wizard' was an excellent tour and details can be found on the informative Six Bells Junction site online – here at Onllwyn the snow and sunshine made for a lovely light for photography as the two class 37s ran round.

The freedom to walk about we were allowed at Onllwyn station was remarkable but quite normal, really, for the period. The fresh footprints in the beautiful snow betray the extent of our wanderings. Also the class 37s were in clean condition and even the buffers had been painted white for the tour. This line had lost its passenger service in 1962 and once ran through to Brecon and on to Hereford via Three Cocks Junction. One aspect of this journey was the number of snow balls thrown by the local youths at our train; well the younger element at one of the stops filled up plastic bags with snow and some lineside throwers got quite a shock when 'fire was returned' from the train! We eventually arrived at Swansea where 50008 took our train back to London and we of course alighted at Reading and had to push my car half the length of the car park to get it going. I had to run alongside and on the fourth time of asking the old dear started at last.

I certainly enjoyed a number of railtours in the 1970s and this was another one to South Wales and again arranged by Railway Pictorial Publications; the organisers enjoyed a bit of alliteration and this one was called 'The Welsh Warrior'. It ran on August 12 1979 from Paddington, with various stops and valley locations on the way. Slough was our departure point, though being a Sunday our train ran late and we had a bit of time to wait. There was a lot of 'special' working about; I noted 47112 on an excursion to York, 47381 on a special to Paignton, 47047 working to Margate and 47265 at the head of a Motorail train. Our train arrived ten minutes down (due off at 08.46) worked by 50046 AJAX and the train seemed a quarter empty. Steve and I had four seats to ourselves in corridor carriage W4767. Passing Swindon we noted a number of 08s outside the Works and my one 'cop' (the law of diminishing returns) of the day 37269 (Landore) the last South Wales based class 37 I needed. At Newport we took the line for Ebbw Vale and from Lime Kiln Junction to Oakdale colliery where AJAX (below) is starting to run round.

A return to Newport and then up the valley to TreThomas for a return to the main line to Cardiff Central where 37176 (Canton) and 37177 (Landore) took over. We travelled right up to Rhymney on a valley line that was still open for passenger traffic and where the two class 37s are shown with 37177 leading. Our time was short here and the BR Staff wanted us out of the way as they had a scheduled train due away at 17.25. We left before this time, back to Cardiff where 50046 was awaiting us for the run back to London. Arrival at Slough was 20.25, more or less on time.

It is December again and once again I was off to South Wales only this time by car on a trip that had been planned for a few weeks with Graham and Ian along, a good old fashioned 'grice' to see how many depots/stabling points we could visit before it got dark. Sunday 7 December 1980 was a good day for us, for by the time we parked in the Service Station on the M4 overlooking the then Severn Road Bridge what had started out a cold winter's day had warmed up and the sun stayed out all day, a boon for photography. We soon found the stabling point at Swansea East Dock and these shunters. They all had their 'targets' for the working week and sat here safe from graffiti; you can see the backs of Graham and Ian – the one in the red jacket with CHAMPION on the back.

There were a few class 37s amid the 08s at East Dock. All were silent, waiting to be started up on Monday morning. Among the lines of locos were 08489, 08577, 08587, 08591, 08658 and 08660 all based at Landore along with 37106 and 37227 of Cardiff and 37304 from Landore.

Margam was not easy to get to and according to the *Locoshed Directory* was 90 minutes walk from Port Talbot station. Under Ian's expert direction we left the M4 at Junction 38, a short way along the A48, right onto the B4283, about 1½ miles a right turn; another right onto a minor road over a level crossing and we were in the depot car park. This modern 'diesel servicing depot' to give it its full original title, was brought into use in March 1964, allowing the immediate closure of Duffryn Yard steam MPD. Its purpose was to service freight locomotives and shunters. Our first sighting was 47151 and a suitably humble inquiry at the supervisors office saw permission granted to roam the depot. It was built within the 180 acre Margam marshalling yard and though only 08s were allocated, there were always main line diesels on shed and sadly like most modern diesel facilities Margam depot is no more. Although we enjoyed the visit we only found nine locomotives today and in the two road shed were 08367 and 08368 both home based, sitting over an inspection pit with a fitter in attendance. Three other 08s on shed were 08578, 08360 and 08362 along with (below) 56035 and 56041; this class was the main object of our expedition to South Wales.

On the same day (Sunday 7 December 1980 to remind you) Canton's 47122 and 47239 were both present and it was a nice surprise to find 45045 COLDSTREAM GUARDSMAN stabled alongside the two road shed and looking rather clean. It was a long way indeed, geographically and operationally, from its London home, Cricklewood. As we got back in the car 47156, another London locomotive, a Stratford class 47, swept past on a four coach train.

Next destination was the stabling point at Radyr. We found the station amid a forest of semaphore signals and courtesy the helpful supervisor we crossed the lines to the stabling point. The sun was in the wrong position but we managed to get a couple of shots in. This one shows 08351 at the head of a line up of 08s which included 08187, 08191 and 08589 all outstationed from Canton. To clear the 08s based there one certainly had to travel round.

There were also two class 37s stabled at Radyr, Canton's 37244 and 37288 both engaged in the main traffic at this time, the coal from a good number of mines then open in South Wales. Of course all this traffic has gone and along with it all the locomotives we saw today.

Well on the way home on the M4 there was time for one more call, Severn Tunnel Junction. Weekends saw a good number of main line diesels lying over before the work started up again on the Monday. It has been recorded that as the local yard was run down there was less work available and Railfreight closed the place in October 1987. There remained a PW store on the site until that too closed in 2002. On arrival we'd parked by the bridge over the main line, underneath which lurked 25248 and 47357; the class 25 a one-time Toton locomotive and the 47 from Crewe.

Walking along the roadway to the depot we got the ok from the Supervisor to look around and with the sun setting in the west I obtained this general view of the diesels on shed. A good line up as well which consisted of: 08361 (then a Margam locomotive), 08582, 08594, 08791, 08948, 08932, 08940, 25297, 37179, 37257, 37277, 37282, 37289, 37308, 45016, 46045, 46053, 47087 CYCLOPS, 47236, 47237, 47262, 47282, 47284, 47324 and 47483. The 08s were all out-based from Ebbw Junction and were of course occupied in the adjacent yard. The main line diesels we saw today came from an assortment of depots: Cardiff, Landore, Crewe, Bristol, Tinsley and Gateshead.

The final photograph of the day shows 08848 and the rather dirty end of the only class 45 on shed, 45016. Nor quite the end of the day for 47551 (Landore) passed by light engine and while having a break sitting in the car 31421, once of Cricklewood, came in on a Cardiff train. The 31 was then based at Bristol.

SCOTLAND

I was able to spend time touring Scotland while holidaying in Co. Durham or during short holidays, always based at Boat of Garten. My diary tells me the first long day trip from Crook was on Sunday 16 July 1978. A year before Don and a friend had done this trip to get around some of the Scottish diesel depots and this encouraged me to do the same. Don shook us awake sharp at 5.00am and three of us were ready to leave at a still-ungodly 6am. It was quite an experience driving north on the A68 from Darlington to Edinburgh especially the blind summits for which I was ill-prepared. This initial Scottish day was very successful and we got around all the depots simply by checking with the Foreman or whoever was on duty. At one shed on a weekend the staff were just signing off and asked us to lock up before we left! In our first weekend in Scotland we stayed at a guest house in Boat of Garten; perfectly, the Strathspey Railway ran alongside the garden. Steve and I had travelled up a few days before. Friday 20 July 1979 saw us sailing over the Forth road bridge, first stop Perth station. There we found 26026 parked in a bay together with an unrecorded 08 shunter and what I presume to be fuel tankers.

40154 (creeping into view above) arrived immediately on an Inverness train. I was quite surprised to find class 40s this far north – it was based at Healey Mills, a long way from Inverness.

Chasing Diesels

This was the most pleasing shot at Perth, three class 26s 'through the fence' stabled for the next day – perhaps this is where the fuel tanks should have been. They turned out to be 26027, 26034 and 26031, all Inverness based. In days of old these inevitably would have been Black 5 4-6-0s.

It was back on the road and heading north on the A9 which in parts were being upgraded to dual carriageway, missing out the centres of population but with no petrol stations so if fuel was required you had to pull into such places as Kingussie or Newtownmore. Our final break was alongside Druimuachdair Summit at 1,484 feet above sea level and we were able to photograph 47469 from Inverness TMD heading south on a MotorRail train, at 4.45pm.

Next day, July 21, we called at Carrbridge station which was quite deserted and rather spoilt by colour light signals. The first movement I saw was a red squirrel hopping over the running lines, to disappear in the adjacent woods. Up and down trains came and went in lousy weather, both class 47 hauled but numbers unrecorded; this is the Perth-bound train.

On Wednesday July 30 1980, once again based at Boat of Garten, we determined on a long drive via Inverness to the Far North, taking in Wick and Thurso. We also went down to Lybster to see if anything remained of the line that once ran from Wick which actually closed to passengers in April 1944. We could find nothing but were obviously looking in the wrong place – in later years it became apparent that Lybster station building still existed, serving as the clubhouse for the local golf course! That aside, first call of the day was Inverness station and local 26019 waiting to depart on a Far North train; that is, to our very destinations.

Road Trips to the Far North

Chasing Diesels

On the way we took in Muir of Ord station, for a Kyle of Lochalsh train was due in at 10.57. We arrived with a few minutes to spare and were nearly surprised by Haymarket's 40064 on a short down goods from the Dingwall direction.

It was pleasing to get two trains at once with the 10.57 headed by 26014 (Inverness, of course) alongside 40064 and its goods. The buildings on the up side were impressive though sadly it was just a bus stop shelter on the other side. Added to the scenery were the semaphores still happily working.

The drive north was somewhat fraught. The weather closed in and at times as we hugged the coast sea mists drifted in to diminish visibility alarmingly. So progress was slow to Helmsdale, the last station before the Far North line turns inland. There was once a two road shed here behind the down platform with the celebrated pair of WR 1600 pannier tanks on the allocation, 1646 and 1649 for the Dornoch branch. We were fortunate to find 26026 (inevitably an Inverness locomotive) in the passing loop at the head of a northbound freight.

Then the 13.29 to Inverness arrived on time with 26043 at its head and I was able to photograph the token exchange with the signalman. A few years later I would be doing the same thing as a volunteer on both the Mid Hants Railway and the West Somerset Railway.

Chasing Diesels

At Georgemas Junction station, the most northerly railway junction in the UK (I believe) we caught up with 26026 shunting the goods train on the Thurso line and 26022 waiting for the down train, which of course split here, to work the Thurso portion of the incoming passenger train from Inverness. I got into conversation with one of the crew from 26026 who had seen us at Helmsdale. They should have been to Wick and back to get the token for the Wick passenger train; the delay was the Royal Train as one of the Royal family had been visiting the area.

The down train duly arrived behind 26046 (Inverness, where else?) the highest numbered of the class which served the Scottish Region very well though soon a good number of their duties were taken over by class 37s. Then off to Thurso for a brief visit but we were able to see 26022 come in on a mixed train for it had some of the wagons that 26026 had brought north.

Because of the bad weather we drove straight back to Inverness and missed out on the 17.45 from there.

Then we were allowed around Inverness depot. Don was hoping for his final two class 26s and one, 26045, was on shed. Great. Though what about 26042? It had worked the 17.45 north from Inverness! This shot of class 26s inside the shed shows how wet the day had been. On shed: 08620, 08728, 25069, 25227, 26018, 26024, 26025, 26035, 26039, 26045, 26046, 27003, 27005, 27008, 27021, 27109, 27204, 40074, 40158 and 47424. The staff were very helpful and one informed us that seven of the class 27s had been transferred to Inverness in recent months whereas there weren't any at all allocated in 1979. It was then back to the guest house and a hot bath for the driver!

On Monday 28 July 1980 we drove to Fort William to ride the train to Mallaig. Our train engine 27022 (then of Eastfield) is backing down on to the Mallaig train. In the lower photo Steve is walking along the Fort William platform, usual carrier bag in hand wanting to record the scene on film. Our train was due out at 13.15 and we left on time. This train had been worked to Fort William (arrival 12.58) by 37026, a former March locomotive now based at Eastfield. 27022 hauled us up to Mallaig, over what has been voted one of the best scenic railway journeys in the world and after today I would not argue with that. This was my first journey over Glenfinnan viaduct (now made famous by the Harry Potter films) with a stop at Glenfinnan station to pass 27038 (another Eastfield locomotive) working the 12.52 from Mallaig. Also attached to our train was the Caledonian Saloon which had joined the train at Fort William though sadly at this time it was in BR livery.

I had to feature this, the old steam shed at Mallaig now looking as if the local fishermen were making use of it. During BR days it was a sub-shed to Fort William. In the 1980s a new road was made to run by the shoreline which sadly involved demolition of this fine stone building.

A different route was taken home which included old stations such as Ballachulish and Bridge of Orchy only to find the trains running late. As we too were running late we calculated we could get to the next station south, Tyndrum Upper, where this photo was taken. It was reached up a track with many pot holes and bends. Again we found another island platform with a passing loop and buildings in pleasant green and white livery, though the train was still late as advised by the chap on duty. It was the 16.35 from Glasgow Queen Street, due in at 18.51 and running forty minutes late, eventually coming in behind 27010. However we were more interested in the class 27 that stood isolated on a separate track at the south end of the station; it had been there since at least the previous Thursday and was 'knackered' we were informed. Our friendly member of staff could not remember the number but as there wasn't another train due for an hour we could walk along the track to get it. Imagine that today! Like 27010, 27210 was also an Eastfield locomotive.

　　　Chasing Diesels

A couple of years later we were back in Scotland and on Monday 16 August 1982 drove to Crianlarich to catch a train to Oban. At Crianlarich the heavens opened in time for us to see the 12.25 from Oban come in on time at 13.38 and I thought this was the time of the train *to* Oban! Motive power was 37039 another one-time March locomotive now shedded at Eastfield. We had to wait until 14.48 (12.55 off Glasgow) for our train which pulled in behind 37027 **LOCH EIL** another former March resident but now part of the Eastfield stud. This shows a crewman ready to do the token exchange.

On arrival at Oban we walked to the other platform and got 37111 alongside our train engine 37027; the former was yet another arrival at Eastfield from March.

Aberdeen Ferryhill

We set off from Boat of Garten on Sunday 22 July 1979 to drive to the East Coast of Scotland and look for closed lines so on, ending up at Fraserburgh where we found the old steam shed intact but minus track and now a play ground for the locals with a thick rope hanging from one of the beams, no doubt used for Tarzan-type amusement. After this came Aberdeen station – no trains but a lovely collection of semaphore signals – then on to Ferryhill depot. The other MPD in the city, Kittybrewster, had been converted to diesels long before Ferryhill but the latter outlasted it by a number of years – Kittybrewster was long gone when we turned up in the Granite City. Strangely, the Ferryhill turntable remained in place, presumably in order to turn the odd vehicle or locomotive for maintenance. It is still there today, with active efforts to bring it onto regular use for engines off specials – or so one hears. This view at Ferryhill included 47206 from Eastfield and 40016, once named CAMPANIA; fuel tanks in the distance indicate how busy the place was.

'Permission to roam' granted as usual, we took our time at Ferryhill, resulting in this close up of the former CAMPANIA. It had begun life working expresses out of Euston in the run-up to electrification but of late, I believed, had been at Kingmoor.

Top. Ferryhill still very much had the look of the steam shed it had been since the Caledonian had built it all those years ago. Latterly, of course, it had attracted visitors from far and wide, in pursuit of A4 and other Pacifics. It stabled main line diesels at this time but had only shunters on its allocation – half a dozen, of which 08515, 08710, 08817 and 08828 were on shed. Ferryhill eventually closed on December 6 1987 and I count myself lucky to have visited it.

Middle. Eastfield class 40 40065 alongside the shed. The depot was an important fuelling point; it was after all, very much 'out on a limb' up in the north east of Scotland.

Bottom. 'On shed' at Ferryhill, Sunday 22 July 1979 and though it only seems like yesterday this photo is now 'historical' for not only have the buildings gone but the class 25s and 40s have not worked for a good number of years. To complete this section, seen on shed this day apart from the four shunters noted above were: 25062 (Inverness), 25082 (Eastfield), 40016, 40065, 40158, 40199, 47015, 47206, 47526 and 47702 SAINT CUTHBERT.

Ayr MPD closed to steam in December 1966 but dmu servicing soldiered on and the typical pattern ensued, fuelling/stabling main line diesels but responsible only for shunters. By the time we paid a visit on Sunday 9 August 1982 the 06s had gone and class 08s were the only diesel locomotives based here. Eventually the depot closed, in 2011 with the tracks lifted in 2014. I had driven north with pal John Stonard for a holiday in Co. Durham with Don and his family though trouble with my fairly new Mini Metro forced us to hire a car for our Sunday trip to Scotland, a Vauxhall Cavalier 1600cc, GHS 954X. Memorable because I managed my first 'ton' in a car as driver – a rite of passage back then and I hope the statute of limitations has expired on that sort of offence if the Police are watching. John in the back was not at all happy it must be said. Anyway, at 6.40am three of us made our way to Dumfries; a quick call in at the station at 9am to find 08601, a Kingmoor-based shunter, on the Stabling Point. Ayr was our first 'proper' depot of the day. As we were armed for once with a permit the Foreman simply waved us in. The depot was set in a triangle of running lines wherein sat 26029 once of Inverness shed, later transferred to Haymarket.

Most main line diesels at Ayr that day were class 20s, like these two alongside the depot; 20156 was an Eastfield resident and doubtless its mate was too. All were coupled like this, nose to nose for working the local coal trains.

The class 20s at Ayr were 20002, 20039, 20111, 20118, 20146, 20156 and 20179, nose to nose. The gentleman in the picture is pal John Stonard dressed for the foul weather we had today. Also on shed were 08345, 08430, 08448 and 08449, 26025, 26020, 26035, 27001, 27105 and 27110. Behind John you can see the modern extension, made to accommodate the dmus. We thanked the Foreman and asked where 08344 was by chance? 'Adrossan Harbour' it transpired so we duly hunted down the missing 08 (I could almost feel the Foreman shaking his head in perplexity behind us) and with this done and the time approaching midday we headed for Glasgow.

Dundee West

The day after our visit to Aberdeen Ferryhill we were on the way back to Co. Durham (July 23 1979) and called in at Dundee with the intention of visiting the diesel depot, known as Dundee West. We shuffled into the Foreman's office and once again got a friendly greeting; we were asked to sign the visitors book and by the way what was the reason for our visit? Photography, sir. The building was the old Caledonian steam shed converted for dmus way back, the North British Tay Bridge shed continued to serve steam until the end.

Remarkably, a dmu trailer car was on the turntable (the second we had encountered this trip) with a class 25 alongside. This was a useful feature as it allowed single cars to be turned in order to make up new pairs in the event of failures or for certain servicing and maintenance requirements.

So far we had noted few locomotives, just 25005 and 27002, both of Eastfield. Haymarket's 40101 then inched out of the shed and behind it we found what we were looking for, the two 06 class diesel shunters based here.

And here they are, 06006 (top) and 06005 below. Also in the shed were 08428, 08712 and 08762. What we also found were two young lads, collecting numbers as we were, all the way from Brighton. The dads were elsewhere but would be back to collect them! We had hoped to find the 06s still extant so this certainly made my day. 06005 was clearly undergoing some sort of maintenance. The little diesels had just the right wheelbase for shunting the local harbour, with one kept as spare.

Dunfermline Townhill

Sunday 27 July 1980 saw us at 'DT', Dunfermline Townhill, the main lure being diesel shunters 06002, 06004 and 06008. I found 06003, 08441 and 08719 in the shed (it was fashioned from an existing wagon works) while lined up outside were 06008, 08175, 08247, 08425, 08726, 20086, 20184, 20206, 20217, 20221, 20223 and 20225. This is the fuelling point with Don walking past one of the filthy class 20s used to haul coal trains to and from the local collieries. The main duties for class 06 was the Kirkcaldy pilot and the Markinch pilot, both stabling weeknights away from DT. This depot finally lost its allocation of class 08s in October 1984 and was eventually demolished in 1989.

Eastfield

Eastfield with its vast allocation was always a favourite during these times. It was a steam shed until November 1965. We caught the depot in its diesel heyday in the early 1980s when it had some 200 locomotives. Despite this, closure came in August 1992 and three years later the buildings were demolished. In the early part of the 21st century a new two road shed was erected near to the site and is used for the servicing and maintenance of modern diesel units. This series of three photographs shows what we could encounter in the early 1980s, beginning with a selection of class 26s in their final years and in the Railfreight livery – 26001 and 26006 of Haymarket shed and 26034 from Inverness. I remember the class before renumbering from the D53XX series as I was lucky to see a few at Kings Cross before they were transferred to Scotland.

A class 47 in ScotRail livery, 47716 (47507) push-pull fitted for the Glasgow-Edinburgh trains and at one timed named DUKE OF EDINBURGH'S AWARD. The Eastfield bloke guiding us round was quite surprised that I took this slide without using a flash. Well I was pleased with the result.

A former class 27 now numbered ADB968028, converted to a static training locomotive. In its former guise as 27027 it had been based at Eastfield having first carried the running number D5374. At the present time it resides at the Caledonian Railway at Brechin.

On Sunday 24 July 1983 we were at Eastfield once again. A couple of months before I had written and got permits for various depots as in the previous year we had found staff a bit less welcoming. The Health and Safety Age was dawning. On this visit we were informed in no uncertain terms, no permit, no visit. A guide was served up – no wandering around by ourselves now. More 37s were appearing in the Scottish Region and 37081, rather work-stained outside the main building, was yet another former March locomotive. It was later named LOCH LONG. From fen to loch you might say. In the background is a snowplough, one of those (if memory serves) fashioned from the tenders of V2 2-6-2s.

One of my favourite photographs, the front ends of a class 20 and class 27s, Sunday 24 July 1983. 'On shed' today were: 08343, 08348, 08402, 08443, 08783, 20002, 20015, 20028, 20045, 20085 late of Toton, 20099, 20118, 20148, 20189, 20201, 27025, 27029, 27032, 27034, 27053, 37012, 37014, 37018, 37022, 37028, 37043, 37081, 37085, 37108, 37190, 37253, 47001, 47160, 47408, 47432 and 47461. Our guide informed us that the large yellow cab ends on the 37s had been done away with after complaints by drivers of light reflection. In store were 40173 and 27043 and on leaving I was asked to put the permit in a small box – I don't know why. On the way out we encountered a permit-less enthusiast who stood no chance of getting past the gate. It was some consolation that the single locomotive he needed was not on shed – we were able to tell him. The stored 27043 was used for re-railing exercises but incredibly *was considered too risky for scrapping because of high asbestos content so it was buried at Patersons Tip, Mount Vernon in Glasgow, 1985.* I can't vouch for the truth of this!

Chasing Diesels

Grangemouth

Grangemouth was opened by the Caledonian Railway in 1908 and still looked very much the steam shed years after being turned over entirely to diesels. It had six dead end roads and a single road repair shop. In 1982 it had just three shunters on its books, 08246, 08561 and 08722 but there were always some main line diesels present. The old place closed in March 1993 and was demolished in 2000. Back in 1984 I wrote: *this depot is near one of the Junctions of the M9 and though only a small shed, it is a must for a visit. The staff are always friendly, the atmosphere is marvellous, well it is an old steam shed, large enough to take about 12 tender engines. I would love to have been there twenty odd years ago.* This is the depot on July 24 1984 with an 08, a class 25 and two class 37s. This was the shed mentioned on page 48, where staff asked us to lock up when we left as they were just going off duty!

We visited Grangemouth on Sunday July 24 1984 and found it nearly deserted with thirteen locomotives stabled: 08196, 08347, 08620, 08722, 08347 new to Grangemouth and me, 20139, 27015, 27046, 27063, 37037, 37148, 37171, 37172 and 37184 once upon a time of Landore. All the class 37s were from Eastfield.

On another visit we once again found a number of class 37s on shed including this one, 37035 an Eastfield locomotive later transferred to Inverness as part of the replacement of the class 26s on the Far North lines.

Parked behind 37035 was 37191 complete with all-round yellow ends, another Eastfield example and another refugee from South Wales, at Landore. It was from this shed of course that locomotives would operate the tanker trains from the nearby Docks and Grangemouth refinery. In 1979 the 08s based here were used 'two in Grangemouth Yard for trips to the docks...one as Stirling station pilot for parcels, coal and seasonal Motorail traffic' while another one was sometimes used at Polmaise Colliery.

Chasing Diesels

Haymarket

Haymarket in the Scottish capital has always been a major depot both steam and diesel. From 1960 class 40s were based here. The Deltics arrived in 1961 and the place closed to steam in September 1963. The modern diesel depot evolved from thereon. 37259 is in the yard outside and the period has to be before the end of 1981 as you can just see a Deltic sneaking into the picture with a goods wagon separating the two locomotives. 37259 was a one-time Stratford class 37 working out of Liverpool Street; later it was at March and Healey Mills.

On Sunday July 24 1984 I had ensured entry by obtaining a permit and this was timed for 10am this Sunday morning. Pleased with ourselves, we presented our permit to the Foreman, bang on 10am. Haymarket lay alongside the main line and we were able to note 47709 THE LORD PROVOST and 47711 GREYFRIARS BOBBY on passing trains. Sadly, now all the Deltics had been withdrawn a bit of the character had gone from this depot though we did find 47712 LADY DIANA SPENCER looking very resplendent.

The brick sidewalls are fragments surviving from Haymarket's steam days. Once we had finished our visit I handed the permit to the Foreman with our thanks and we headed for Grangemouth. Unlike most depots we visited in the 1980s Haymarket is still open, servicing dmus and as a recent publication has noted 'it has a secure future for many years to come.'

Inverness

We awoke at the Ryvoan Guest House, Boat of Garten, on Saturday July 21 1979 to a dull, overcast morning but to a very substantial breakfast which set us up for the day. This was courtesy the lovely landlady Mrs Harrower, alas no longer with us. Just after 9am we headed for Inverness; on the station we had easy access to the platforms and my first shot shows 26039 waiting to depart on a Far North train. At this period the class 26s dominated the lines to Kyle of Lochalsh and Wick and Thurso and as you can see it was rather wet. 26039 was one of the class fitted with double headlights for operating north of Inverness. From the end of this platform we noted 20039 and 20149 on shed; thus encouraged and having got this far, we walked off the end of Platform 5 and into the depot where we received a friendly greeting from the Foreman. Looking back all these years later, with razor wire and security guards, this seems incredible – we were after all, trespassers, not to beat about the bush. He was happy for us to wander round. The buildings had been converted from the former Lochgorm Works and in the 21st Century still has some 08s on allocation. Latterly it has been home to class 158 and 170 diesel units.

Inside the converted works, forming the most northerly diesel depot in the kingdom. We felt privileged to be allowed round and the three of us spent a good hour taking photographs. Note the class 26 at the head of the line up still carries its mini snow ploughs; they were yellow and the paint was fresh.

The depot, then coded IS with a mix of class 20, 25, 26 and 47. At one time a number of class 47s were allocated, including 47464, 47467, 47469, 47474, 47546 and 47550 and these would have been used to Aberdeen and down the main line to Perth and further south.

One of the IS class 26s on July 21 1979. They were mainly for the Far North lines though more than once I've caught them double heading passenger trains to Perth. Note the full yellow ends, twin headlights, a disc panel displayed with three more available for head codes and two red lights for use if the diesel was at the end of the train or running as a light engine. At one time a more or less complete run of 26s could be found at Inverness: 26008, 26010-26015, 26018, 26019, 26021-26046 and in my travels I am pleased to say that I saw all of them.

Class 26s parked up on July 21 1979, two still with snow ploughs fitted. Seen on shed today (as written down) were 20020, 20121, 26012, 47427, 26043, 26036, 26024, 26019, 26040, 26025, 25007, 47706, STRATHCLYDE, 47469, 26030, 26021, 26033, 26041, and 20179. Busying themselves around the yards were 08568 and 26035 which eventually departed on a train to Kyle. At the station were 08568 and 08620.

A pair of class 20s at Inverness, nose to nose as usual. In the background is one of the typical signal boxes that could then be seen in the Inverness area. One of the duties for the class 20s was block trains of alumina wagons for the smelter at Invergordon. On leaving the depot we thanked the Foreman and stayed to see 47706 on a Perth-bound departure.

Back on the station 26019 was waiting to work a Far North train; the weather having improved during our shed visit.

Millerhill

Millerhill was one of the few new diesel depots built in Scotland, constructed to serve the new Millerhill Marshalling Yard. It had a single road and fuelled the diesels working in. Originally an outstation of St Margarets in Edinburgh that finished when the parent shed shut. It never had an allocation but was coded MH by British Rail and during our visits had a number of Haymarket locomotives 'on shed' especially some of the class 26s. On July 16 1978, driving around parts of Scotland, Edinburgh to Glasgow and back and on the return we decided to pay a brief visit to Millerhill. Again permission was readily forthcoming though building-wise there was little to see. This line of class 26s was made up of 26001, 26002, 26004 and 26005, all then based at Haymarket.

This would be practically the entire stud of Millerhill's shunters; 08564, 08711, 08714, 08734 and 08789, all out-based from Haymarket.

I was surprised at how many class 40s were based in Scotland, for back in the early 1960s I had got used to seeing them in the London area. This one at Millerhill is 40165 with 40142 behind the class 47. Although July 16 1978 was a Sunday we had two goods train pass by while looking round, 25085 and 26003 both from Haymarket.

An undated photograph (though it would have been a summer Sunday) taken on a later visit to Millerhill – provision was not lavish!

Millerhill with a different line up of locomotives including 37s and 47s. The shed was modern but a cash-conscious Scottish Region (it built very little brand new for its diesels) still made use of the traditional grounded van body.

During another visit to Millerhil we found 47604 isolated on a stub of track at Millerhill; at one time it carried the name WOMEN'S ROYAL VOLUNTARY SERVICE, bestowed in 1988. Millerhill was operated by both EWS and DB after privatisation but closed in 2016. The building was reported demolished (it wouldn't have taken much) by September that year.

In the times I visited the Scottish depots all those years ago Motherwell was one was my favourites; it positively oozed atmosphere. This was a typical line up whenever we went there. One of the major depots in Scotland during my visits it always had an allocation of 08s, 20s, and 37s. The class 20s were used on ballasts and MGR trains from the local collieries to Longannet power station and the class 37s on trains to and from the great steelworks at Ravenscraig.

Another undated view; two class 37s alongside the shed, one in BR livery the other in the later Railfreight grey and both fitted with twin head codes. This was a set of lines you crossed over from the supermarket car park to get in to the depot. The dear old *Shed Directory* never had to feature a supermarket in its directions – perish the thought – though more than one of its sheds ended up demolished to make way for one...

I had to use this photograph of July 16 1978 because it features my good friend Don in his element, photographing diesels at which he was quite adept. It also shows the fine stonework of the shed building – highly unusual I'd think, to see dressed stone used for an engine shed, on this scale at least. Cleaning it would be a job – decade after decade of soot from steam engines overlain with endless diesel exhaust. The interior still has a gloomy look despite a set of modern lighting.

Alongside Motherwell depot this day we found 27007 and the depot breakdown crane, all set to go probably. This class 27 was then based at Eastfield. I'm pleased to say the building still stands and in 2011 Network Rail let it to Direct Rail Services who then used it for wagon maintenance. A number of details quoted in this Scottish depot section is thanks to *Railways of Britain On Shed. 5: The Scottish Region* published in 2019 which in the bibliography lists *Shed by Shed 1982 edition* of which I was co-author.

Chasing Diesels